all about KOTOR

KOTOR CITY GUIDE

BRANKO BANJO CEJOVIC

Author: Branko BanjO Cejovic

Cover design by Olivera Cejovic
Part of text by Danilo Lekovic
Latest editing & translation by: Jack Taylor
Book design & Photos by Branko BanjO Cejovic

Published by Visit-Montenegro.com
Distributed by BritishDotCom ltd

First Edition: January 2013
Last Edition: Jun 2014

ISBN-13: 978-1496108562
ISBN-10: 1496108566

Content

Kotor

Montenegro Coast

Located along one of Montenegro's most beautiful bays is Kotor, a city of traders and famous sailors, with many stories to tell. The Old City of Kotor is a well preserved urbanization typical of the middle Ages, built between the 12th and 14th century. Medieval architecture and numerous monuments of cultural heritage have made Kotor a UNESCO listed "World Natural and Historical Heritage Site". Through the entire city, the buildings are crisscrossed with narrow streets and squares.

One of these squares contains the Cathedral of Saint Tryphon (Sveti Tripun), a monument of Roman culture and one of the

most recognizable symbols of the city. The Church of Saint Luke (Sveti Luka) from the 13th century, Church of Saint Ana (Sveta Ana) from the 12th century, Church of Saint Mary (Sveta Marija) from the 13th century, Church of the Healing Mother of God (Gospe od Zdravlja) from the 15th century, the Prince's Palace from the 17th century and Napoleon's Theatre from the 19th century are all treasures that are part of the rich heritage of Kotor. Carnivals and festivals are organized each year to give additional charm to this most beautiful city of the Montenegrin littoral.

You simply can not afford to miss a visit to Kotor. There are also two other places near Kotor that we highly recommend to visit:

Perast

Perast is a sleepy Baroque town near Kotor. The most beau-

tiful buildings of this small city were built in the 17th and 18th centuries. At the time seafaring was growing and captains built magnificent villas that even today capture you with their beauty. Perast is a quiet and peaceful place. It abounds in sacred monuments, such as the Church of Saint Nicola (Sveti Nikola) built between the 15th and 17th centuries, the Parish church build in 1740, the island in front of Perast where the church Saint George (Sveti Djordje) from the 12th century is located, and the Church of Our Lady of the Rock (Gospa od Skrpjela) build in 1630, a church built in the Baroque style on top of an artificial island.

Risan

The oldest city of the Bay of Kotor, Risan, originated in the 3rd century BC and was the seafaring, commercial and workshop centre of the Illyrian State. With the arrival of the Romans in Risan, palaces were built with the best Greek marble and decorated with magnificent sculptures and mosaics. These have lasted up to the present and form an invaluable cultural treasure. Among the large number of mosaics is one of the God Hypnos, which is remarkable in that it is the only known mosaic figure of the God of Dreams.

History

Even though we are now in the XXI century, the science has still, unfortunately, not yet established when the first lodgment in Kotor was founded. The earliest mention of Kotor is found in historical records that date back to Classical Antiquity. According to some other data Kotor is two millennia old and its name stems from the word DEKATERA (from ancient Greek 'KATAREO' – meaning HOT). The written sources mention the "Upper town", which referred to the oldest part of the lodgment on the top of the hill Sveti Ivan (St. Ivan) (above Kotor), and the "Lower town", present Kotor.

The rich history of Kotor is parallel to the rich culture of the town with which many conquerors ruled: the Illyrians, the Venetians, the Austrians, the French …

First, the town was ruled by the Illyrians (III and II century BC). On the other hand, the Romans are considered to be the founders of Kotor 168 BC – 476 AD Kotor was under their reign until the break of Roman Empire in 476 AD. After the Romans and until the year 1185, Kotor was under the reign of Byzantium. Instead of Akruvijum, as Kotor was then named, under the Byzantium reign Kotor is named DEKADERON.

In the period from 1185 – 1371 Kotor remains one of the coastal towns which are a part of the Medieval Serbian state, under the management of dynasty Nemanjic. The dynasty Nemanjic names the town Kotor, and they make Kotor a seaport, through which they have maintained connections with the west. During the reign of the Serbian dynasty Nemanjic Kotor experiences a significant economic as well as cultural boon.

After the Nemanjic dynasty, Kotor is taken over by the Hungarians. The Hungarian King Ludvik rules Kotor from 1371 to 1384. After that, Kotor was governed by Bosnian King Tvrtko I (1384 – 1391).

During the period from 1391 to 1420 Kotor was an independent Republic. Because of the threat of the Turks conquering the town, in 1420 the people from Kotor voluntarily, and in accordance with the decision of the Big Council of Kotor, give the management of the town to the Venetian Republic, which lasted until 1797. Considering the fact that at this time Kotor was a battle field, the period until 1797 is thought to be the most dramatic and the hardest in the history of Kotor.

The history of Kotor also notes natural catastrophes with several earthquakes having hit Kotor. There were earthquakes in 1537, 1563, 1667, 1729 and 1979. Kotor also survived the years when the world was infested with a contagious disease – the plague in 1422, 1427, 1457, 1467 and 1572.

From 1797 to 1805 Kotor was a part of the Austrian empire. In 1806 the Russians came to Kotor. They governed the town only for a year – until 1807.

The French soon began to menace Kotor. As the Russian army was defeated by the French in the battle near Fridland, the Russians, with a secret contract, gave Kotor to France, which ruled over Kotor from 1807 until 1813.

In September of 1813 the Montenegrin ruler Petar I Petrovic helped the people from Kotor. The Montenegrins and the people from Boka (another name for Kotor) fought together against the French Monarchy. At that time Boka and Montenegro became united.

However, that unison lasted for only nine months, because the Paris Peace Congress, which was held in 1814, did not acknowledge the unison. After that conference, Boka with its surroundings was given to Austria (1814 – 1918).

The one hundred year reign of Austria over Kotor was marked by numerous rebellions and uprisings of the people from Boka Kotorska.

Kotor's liberation from Austria finally came in 1918.

As with all other towns of the former Kingdom of Serbs, Croats and Slovenians, Kotor - exhausted by the numerous occupations - awaited the biggest war ever fought – WWII, in the year 1941.

Kotor experienced liberation from Nazi control in November 1944.

Legend

Almost every part of Kotor, every stone with which its streets are paved and its palaces that surround certain parts of the town are built, is a monument that can tell a very nice story, a true story or a nonsense story.

Already when we pronounce the word Kotor, we immediately recollect other parts (lodgments), which are also parts of Kotor like: Perast, Prcanj, Risan, Dobrota etc

So whilst we are mentioning Dobrota, here is a story about its foundation:

Two travelers, who were traveling around the world, came to the grey sea. As they were already exhausted from the long trip, they sat on some kind of a rock to get some rest and to refresh themselves. One of them moved a little bit to one side and noticed a plaque with some inscription on it. The inscription said: "Measure 10 lengths dig and stop". When they read that, they wondered what could that be, so they started to guess together what that instruction could mean. At one moment, they came to an idea to measure 10 lengths with the plaque and so they did. When they measured the required lengths, they started to dig a small hole in the ground and they found some kind of a small chest. They tried to open it, but to their astonishment, the chest opened by itself.

At the bottom of the chest and with golden letters was written "this is for everyone's goodness". For a long time they thought what they should do?! Whether to stay where they are or to continue with their journey? Still, as the message was like some kind of a vow,

they stayed in the place where they have found the message. At the same place, they quickly made a cottage and went to sleep.

During the night, something very strange happened. From

the wooden chest, some new shiny letters glimmered. The new message said: "Wish whatever you want before sleep"! As both of the travelers from the beginning of the story were poor, they wished for nice stone houses and beautiful wives. When they woke up in the morning, they were speechless. They saw a white castle and a woman in the window looking towards the sea. They immediately moved into this new home and continued to live in ease. Since that, every night before they went to sleep, they wished for another nice house and every morning one emerged.

That is how Dobrota, near Kotor, was founded.

Stone houses and numerous palaces, which were built later, are the most beautiful details of Dobrota.

Culture

Kotor is surely the most famous Montenegrin town when we are talking about culture and cultural landmarks. At the end of XIX century, Kotor, in the bay of Boka Kotorska or the southern fjord, as that bay is now called because of its unsurpassed beauty, got the epithet of "Bride of the Adriatic".

Its amazing beauty comes from the blue sea, the stony shore, the slopes of the most famous Montenegrin Mountain – Lovcen - and the greenery, which with the rocks above the bulwarks of Old Kotor creates unusual natural colors. Its beauty is also created by the serpentines toward the fortresses of San Djovani (St. Giovanni) or Sveti Ivan (St. Ivan). These medieval palaces, the old town, the unavoidable and the always cheerful spirit of inhabitants, from whatever nation or religion they are.

Kotor has been a challenge for every tourist for centuries. Not so much in the sense of tourism, as it was challenging as a town of great cultural value with monuments of culture from the past, like its churches and cathedrals are. On every step that takes you through the Old Kotor town you can, for a while at least, through imagination, go back to the Middle century, the Baroque age or the period when the pirates reined the world's coasts. If you are for the first time in Kotor, the impression that you will have, we are sure, will be more convincing that the adventures from the movies that you have seen, or the books that you have read about those ages, or about this town. It has the tracks of the Illyrian and Roman cultures, as well as pre-Roman, Gothic, Renaissance and Baroque culture. Kotor Old Town is included with the Mediterranean towns that have the best preserved medieval urban settlements from the XII to XIV century and since 1979, it is included in the list of the world cultural heritage under the protection of UNESCO.

The medieval town Kotor is situated on the very end of the Bay of Boka Kotorska. Today Kotor is the biggest old urban settlement in Montenegro. The oldest archeologically noted edifice that originates from the VI century AD is the early Christian Basilica found below the church of Sveta Marija Koledjate (St. Maria Koledjate) or Gospa od zdravlja (Virgin of Health) in the immediate vicinity of the main town doors of the Old Kotor. Already in the XI century, Kotor got its protector, Sveti Tripun (St. Tripun), in whose honor the cathedral, which is today considered to be a symbol of Kotor, was being built.

The cultural richness of Kotor is invaluable. The treasury of the town hides the most significant cultural monuments like: Sat Kula (Watch Tower) from the VIII century, Cathedral of Sveti

Tripun (St. Tripun) from the XII century, Church of Sveti Luka (St. Luke) from the XII century, the Prince's palace from the XVII century, Church of Sveta Marija (St. Maria) from the XII century, Church of Gospa od zdravlja (Virgin of Health) from the XV century and Napoleon's Theater from the XIX century.

Kotor is surrounded by the town bulwarks, that is, the walls around the town, the walls above the town and the walls around the hill as well as the fortress Sveti Djovani (St. Ivan) on the top of the hill with the same name.

No matter which doors or entrance into Old Kotor you are coming through, the asymmetrical structure of the narrow streets and squares has numerous medieval monuments. Not just monumental edifices like the churches, cathedrals or museum monuments, but also with the ornaments of the historical and ordinary edifices, like family houses in which people still live. On the large number of family houses it is still easy to notice the marks of the past epochs. Mostly those are ornaments that usually testify to the Roman Empire in these territories. You can see Roman marks, like numbers, sentences, lion characters, dragons, snakes etc… All around you can see Baroque windows, big walls with richly and skillfully decorated arches.

In Kotor there are also numerous palaces: palace Drago, with Gothic windows from the XV century; palace Bizanti from the XII century; palace Pima, with typical shapes of renaissance and Baroque, from the XVI century; palace Grubonja, with a coat of arms of the Old Kotor pharmacy, founded in 1326 year; palace Grgurin from the XVII century, which today is the building of the Maritime Museum, as well as the Sat kula (Clock tower) dating from the XVI century, beside which there is a medieval pillory.

Historians mostly agree with the fact that the most important period for Kotor was the period of medieval centuries and that is because Kotor experienced a great economic boon at that time. The strongly developed economy soon influences the development of education and extremely good progress of culture, art and construction. Already from the end of the XIII century, in Kotor, we have a grammatical school from which a multitude of humanistic writers and scientists emerged. The first humanistic writers are mentioned on the transition from XV to the XVI century. We don't know much about them, so the works that they have authorized were not preserved. Without any doubt though, the most famous poet was Bernard Pima, the descendant of the old and widely famous Kotor noble family Pima. Only a few of his verses in Latin, written in the Ciceron language, were preserved. Then we also have a Kotor nobleman, from the end of the XV century and the first decades of the XVI century, Trifun Bizanti and Kotor's patrician brothers Vicko and Dominiko Buca. As a printer and a book editor, among the more famous ones is Lord Jerolim Zagurovic.

When we are talking about the Renaissance literature it is good to mention Djordje Bizanti, who already in 1532 in Venice printed the verses in Italian and Latin. Still, the most fruitful Renaissance poet was Ludovik Pakvalic (1500 -1551) from Kotor. With the previous two, the poet Ivan Bona Borilis also marked the XVI century. Theological writers also have marked Kotor. One of the most significant was Luka Bizanti who governed the Kotor church for 4 decades.

Especially developed in that time in Kotor, was the art of

cultivation (processing) of metals and stone, which made the Kotor masters famous all over Europe. Also famous is constructor and Kotor master Vito Trifunov or Vito from Kotor – a monk of a smaller church. According to some Kotor documents during 1326

and 1327 fray Vito constructed the famous monastery Visoki De-cani (High Decani) in Serbia.

In the middle century in Kotor the so-called Greek painters worked. Among them were Nikola and Manojlo who painted at the beginning of the XV century. In the XIII and XIV century Kotor had its own pharmacy and doctors, goldsmiths, gun blacksmiths and smithy, library, classical education, theologians and a communal or-ganization of the town, Statute, notary books... More than 5 centu-ries ago in Kotor a famous shopkeeper Marin Drusko lived. It is also worth mentioning the name of the famous trader and Kotor captain Marko Grgurovic.

Still, without any doubt, the greatest number of famous peo-ple from Kotor came from Perast, a place close to Kotor, which also has a lot of famous palaces. Among the famous people from Perast is Andrija Paltasic, a printer and editor (1450 – 1500), who worked in Venice from 1477 to 1493. From the Zmajevic family came the

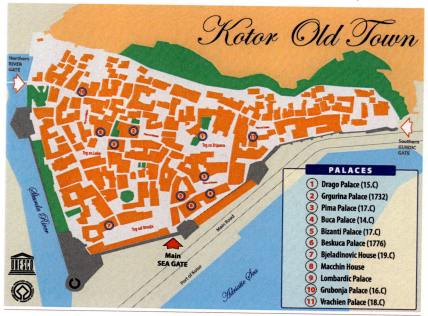

Kotor Old Town

PALACES

1 Drago Palace (15.C)
2 Grgurina Palace (1732)
3 Pima Palace (17.C)
4 Buca Palace (14.C)
5 Bizanti Palace (17.C)
6 Beskuca Palace (1776)
7 Bjeladinovic House (19.C)
8 Macchin House
9 Lombardic Palace
10 Grubonja Palace (16.C)
11 Vrachien Palace (18.C)

writer and Archbishop of Bar, Andrija Zmajevic (1624 – 1694) and Vicko Zmajevic (1670 – 1745), a church politician and a writer...

The most famous representative of the well–known Kotor painting is the painter Tripo Kokolja (1661 – 1713) whose works of art are decorating the little church on the Island Gospa od Skrpjela. This painter became famous in most in the entire Mediterranean.

The end of the XVII century is also an interesting epoch in the history of Kotor. It was marked by the collaboration of certain people from Kotor, especially from Perast in the Morej war (1684 – 1699) and a very distinguished personality of that period, Vicko Bujovic, as well as the famous seaman from Perast, Matija Zmajevic, who later became the Russian Empire Admiral.

The most famous Kotor seaman and the captain though is Ivo Vizin. In 1852, by going on a usual trading journey, with his small sailboat the Splendido - from which a very nice hotel in Morinj near Kotor got its name - Vizin made the biggest naval project of the XIX century: by cruising from harbor to harbor, he sailed the world.

Long before Vizin, more precisely in 1823, a navigational officer Stevan Vukotic is being mentioned. Along with the names of Vizin and Vukotic, the history of Kotor remembers several other well–known seamen and captains like Petar Zambelic and Marko Ivanovic.

The collector of national treasures and folklore Vuk Vrcevic (1811 – 1882) was born in Kotor.

In the surroundings of Kotor, more precisely in the area known as Grbalj, the Archbishop of Cetinje and Metropolitan of

Montenegro, Mitrofan Ban (1841 – 1920), was born.

Even in history that is more recent there are famous people from Kotor. A world-known man from Kotor today is Tripo Simonuti, a violinist and a free artist, born in 1932. With his daughters Ana and Irena he founded a chamber trio which is well known outside the borders of Montenegro under the name "Trio Simonuti".

Dr Milos Milosevic lives and works in Kotor. He is the current Boka Navy Admiral.

It is also important to mention a former professor in the Maritime Faculty as well as in the Faculty of Tourism, Milenko Pasinovic and violinist Ratimir Martinovic, who both work and live in Kotor.

Nature

Boka Kotorska is situated in the south eastern part of the Adriatic Sea. The south east side of Boka Kotorska is surrounded by the limestone massifs of the mountain Lovcen (1749 m) and from the north west by the slopes of the mountains Orjen (1895 m), Radostak (1446 m) and Dobrostica (1570 m).

Near Kotor are two peninsulas, on the north-west side is the Vitaljinsko peninsula and on the south east side is Lusticko peninsula. These two peninsulas are separated by the Ostro Stait, which is the point of greatest protrusion into the bay of Boka Kotorska.

Nearby there are two further peninsulas, Vrmacko and Devesinjsko, which are separated by the Verige gorge. That gorge further divides the bay of Boka Kotorska into two inner bays, Risan and Kotor bay and on the two outer bays, Tivat and Topalj bay.

Experts in the protection of the human environment and urban areas agree that the territory of Boka Kotorska, viewed as a geo–morphological and vegetative–geographical entity, is very rich in nature. When we are talking about those characteristics, we also need to mention an unusual contrast of relief, the remains of the tectonic disturbances, lime surfaces, as well as the deciduous vegetation in the very coastal zone.

Kotor is situated on the narrow plateau under Lovcen, on the east side of the Kotor Bay. Its center is made of the Old town, which is surrounded by 4,5 km long bulwarks that stretch from the sea along the hill slopes of Sveti Ivan up to the fortress on the top. On the west side, along the shore, in the foothill of the hill Vrmac, we have lodgments Muo, Prcanj, and Stoliv, and in the east Dobro-ta, Orahovac, Perast, and Risan. Kotor Municipality also has one part of the Grbalj field, which is found in the south east of the bay. Together with the Upper Grbalj it goes out in the open sea. Near the cove Jaz, Kotor borders with Budva.

The summers in Kotor are warm and dry and the winters mild and humid. The average annual temperature is around 15 °C. For 213 days in the year, there is no wind and the swimming season lasts for 144 days. This climate has a distinct effect on the development of vegetation in Kotor. Considering the fact that it spreads from the Adriatic Sea and the karst background, the area of Boka Kotorska is found under the influence of both the Mediterranean and mountain climate. When those two types of climate meet and mix, a special kind of the sub-Mediterranean climate is created. Not only the climate but also the sea in the Bay of Boka Kotorska is of great importance. The sea by Kotor acts as the accumulator of warmth and the source of water vapor, which is one of the most important factors along with the temperature circulation and the amount of rain in the entire area of Boka Kotorska. Kotor spreads over the area of 335 km2. With the sub-Mediterranean climate, the average air temperature in January is around 7 °C whilst in July it is about 23 °C.

The unique beauty of the Kotor Bay is also expressed by the stone houses and captain's palaces, which you can see along the shore of Kotor, as well as with the contrast of the sea and steep high mountains.

The bay of Boka Kotorska is the most southern fiord in the world. It is made up of four bays: Kotor, Risan, Tivat, and Herceg

Novi bay. Its total surface is 84 km2 the maximum depth is 60m and the total length of the shore is 106 km.

The climate in Kotor is sub-tropic. Not only during the winter, but also in the Fall and in the Spring the rains are heavy. In the far end of the bay of Boka Kotorska, in the place called Crkvice, there is yearly 5,317 mm of rain per square meter, which is the maximum of rainfall in Europe.

Whether you're coming to Kotor in the summer or in the winter, the picture of the Kotor landscape will catch your attention. The summer picture would be — mountains surrounding the Kotor bay that are reflecting themselves in the clear blue sea, precisely brimmed with the sunbeams or the winter one which would be the slopes of green mountains partially or completely covered with snow and along the Kotor shore you can smell the mixture of scents of citrus fruits, oranges, various flowers like mimosa, camellia or other Mediterranean plants, whose seed for centuries have been traveling by sail boats and ships from the farthest spots on the globe to Kotor, Risan, Perast, Stoliv or Dobrota.

In the majority of coastal towns in Kotor you can also see various types of palm trees. Outside the Kotor bulwarks on the way towards Dobrota, on both sides, you will see palm trees. The slopes of the mountains are covered with cypress, pine, oak and beech forests. Wild and domestic pomegranate, figs, oranges, mandarins, grape, and olive can also be spotted there. Numerous front gardens of family houses and often the abandoned Kotor palaces have Mediterranean plants. Besides the palm trees, there are various types of cactus, oleander, mimosa, magnolia, camellia and other kinds of Mediterranean plants which were brought there along with the trophies of victory from great maritime battles. Kotor traders and seaman brought them as a symbol of beauty and remain synonyms of Kotor even today.

The Bay of Boka Kotorska is a rich fishing ground and part of the population of Kotor makes a living from it. They catch mostly white fish like surmullet (Lat.mullus barbatus), sea perch (Lat. Dicentrarchus labrax), bogue (Lat. Boop boops) whilst the more skilful and persistent fisherman can often catch the expensive white fish san pier (Lat Zeus faber).

But also leer fish (Lat. Lichia amia), Atlantic bonito (Lat. Sarda sarda) and in past times there have been a lot of pilchards (Lat. Sardine pilchardus), which today are pretty much extinct and it is becoming harder and harder to find it even in the famous Kotor market.

In Kotor, there are also several private cultivators of mussels and shells. Those growing places are situated next to the very stony shore. The majority of private managers from the mentioned growing places supply mostly their own restaurants, hotels and motels with these very tasteful sea products.

Throughout the year, many cruise ships as well as luxurious yachts visit Kotor harbor. In recent years, Kotor has been receiving an increasing number of foreign visitors.

Farther down the coast, towards Dobrota and Perast, along with the stony shore, we can see anchored barges. On the azure blue sea you can often see gulls and swallows and smaller birds, while in the countryside behind Kotor, mostly in the hills, that surround the town, you can also see foxes, rabbits, squirrels, wild pigs and others…

Tourism – Beaches

When we are talking about beaches, the whole of Boka Bay, including Kotor, hardly has any sandy beaches like in other part of the Montenegro Coast.

Considering the fact that it is mainly a town of the extraordinary cultural value, Kotor has for centuries developed in that direction. The culturally – historical town of Kotor has several stony beaches that are mostly in front of hotels and there may be two or three rows of easy chairs with parasols. The summers are warm and dry whilst the winters are mild and humid. The average annual temperature is around 15 °C. Some 200 days in a year are without any wind and the swimming season lasts for 140 days in a year. Two small sandy beaches, with very small capacities, are found in Orahovac and Ljuta and they are several kilometers away from the center of the town, on the way towards Risan.

You can also find smaller cafés situated along the stony shore or along the lower part of the main road in Kotor that offer summer refreshments with various juice drinks and visitors are offered easy chairs for sunbathing and umbrellas, as well as swimming in the waters of Bay of Boka Kotorska.

Should the nature itself as well as Kotor charm you that much that there is no reason for you to spend your vacation in some other town on the Montenegrin coast, then we are convinced that you will manage with the swimming and sunbathing in Kotor. After all, almost every visitor or guest of Kotor will easily confirm that the refreshment from the summer heat is simple even in Kotor.

Actually, if the enjoyment and relaxing in the sea is most important to you, then we can say that Kotor with its stony shore – instead of real beaches – is an ideal place for you. If you follow this short rule, you will easily have a good rest. Here is how you're going to do that: bring a bottle of water and a big towel with you, find a part of the stony shore that is reasonably smooth, sit for a while to prepare yourself, then jump into the water, have a nice swim, come back and dry yourself. After that, observe the far blue shores, away from the murmur of other swimmers and enjoy the peace of which you dreamt in the big town from which you have come.

Tourism - Hotels

Kotor has a number of great hotels with some of them amongst the best in Montenegro. You can also find some really unique hotels in Old Town of Kotor.

Almost all hotels in Kotor have the necessary tourist standards and they fulfill the criteria of the modern tourists and guests. Most of them have their own parking lots, open and indoor pools and halls for various types of recreation, gardens for rest or lunch, rent-a-car service etc. The hotels along the sea shore have also the improvised mostly stone beaches on which you can relax in easy chairs under hotel parasols. Should you decide to spend your summer vacation in Kotor, then guests mostly spend their holiday in these hotels: "Splendido", "Teuta", Fjord" or "Vardar".

Five Kotor hotels at the moment have two stars, there are several hotels with three stars and only one hotel facility has earned four stars.

The most comfortable, according to the marks of the commission for hotel keeping and the most beautiful of all Kotor hotels, is Hotel "Splendido", which has four stars and is situated in Prcanj, close to Kotor. That hotel was built quite recently. It got the name "Splendido" from the sailing boat of the same name. It was the sailing boat of the famous Kotor seamen Ivo Vizin, who became famous by his accomplishment from the XIX century, sailing around the world.

If you are interested in a more private arrangement then there are a number of smaller hotels as well as houses and apartments for rent. It is estimated that there are several hundred private renting options. Private accommodation is mostly advertised through private tourist agencies or by Internet. The prices in those facilities can be much lower when compared to the hotel prices.

Tourists for whom comfort, along with exclusivity and enjoyment, is the first priority have at their disposal numerous villas, either newly built or those that used to be magnificent edifices or palaces for the reception of guests.

Featured Hotels in Kotor:

1. Hotel "Forza Mare", Dobrota
2. Hotel "Vardar", Old Town
3. Hotel "Palazzo Radomiri", Old Town
4. Hotel "Splendio", Prcanj
5. Hotel "Hippocampus", Old Town

Tourism - Food and Drink

The most typical Mediterranean cuisine, as the national cuisine in Montenegro was originally called, can be found in Kotor. There isn't a restaurant, open terrace, hotel terrace or Kotor fiesta which doesn't serve Kotor specialties. We are suggesting that as soon as you come to Kotor you try the domestic fish thick soup (usually prepared from cooked trout). That is actually one type of fish soup, with pieces of fish, as well as rice and various condiments, that give the meal a dark red color and an exciting scent which lures you to try that meal, even if you are not a great fish fan.

When it comes to sweet treats the people of Kotor will give you "frustula" (a crunchy, dry, sweet cookie of rhombus shape), but the most famous meal is Kotor's "njoke" (a pasta specialty), which is mostly served during the big and famous Kotor carnival.

Besides the traditional Montenegrin cuisine, which is made with smoked ham, cheese, olives complemented by local red and white wines, in Kotor you can find all other kinds of specialties. In almost every hotel, restaurant or café you can order all kinds of Italian pizzas as well as other Italian specialties.

On the menus of most Kotor hotels and restaurants you can also find all kinds of fish specialties and meals that are made of the fruits of the sea: octopus salad, rice with sea fruits, fish thick soups, lobsters, grilled squids, various kinds of sea fish etc...

Because the cuisine in Kotor is mostly Mediterranean, with almost all fish specialties, cooks use condiments that make the aroma and taste of the Mediterranean cuisine even more special. Those are: lemon, parsley, basil, rosemary, garlic, as well as other spices that make the meal healthy and tasteful.

Your enjoyment and impression about Kotor will reach a peak after only one day spent in Kotor, as you sum up your impressions from some of its hotels or restaurants, trying out one after another specialty and delicacies that you didn't know existed.

Featured Restaurant in Kotor:

1. **G**alion
2. **B**ocalibre
3. **P**alazzo

Tourism - Shopping

In the interior of the Old Kotor is the largest number of shops and boutiques. There you can also find smaller shops and vendors that are offering footwear and clothes of renowned European and world designers and creators. The larger boutiques offer almost all pieces of fashion clothes of Italian fashion designing firms. The appearance and offers in these boutiques are of a very high level. Kotor boutiques give the appearance of the harmony in the choice of patterns of the clothes, material and they show us the skill of the trading, as if it were a craft, which has for years been done in the Old Town. In the Kotor shops consumers of all ages and tastes can find almost everything that is necessary for a nice, decent and modern appearance.

Besides the boutiques and shops for clothes, in the Old Town you also can find a great number of souvenir shops, photo shops, jewelry shop, book shops, antique shops, shops of mixed goods, hairdresser saloons and beauty saloons, barber shops, cafés, pizzerias, pastry shops etc...

By the second entrance into the Old Town, just across the Kotor Riva and harbor, you can find the Kotor bazaar or market. Since forever that place was intended for the exchange and barter of various goods and merchandise. Today though that market sells mostly fruits, vegetables and fish, but there are some stands with costume jewelry and other inevitable market trinkets.

Several hundred meters further, on the right side, there is a bigger department store, in which you have a larger number of boutiques and shops. In almost every part of Kotor you can find a great number of food stores and super markets.

Also, you can visit the smaller shopping center of Kamelija, near to the Old City. This shopping center offers a wide range of very nice shops and a couple of restaurants and cafes.

Tourism – Activities

If you are looking for an ideal place to rest from the fast pace of life, then a visit to Kotor is mandatory. Morning life in the Old Town is relaxed and calm with many people enjoying their coffee or tea in one of the many terraces or café bars. In the evening, the Old Town fills up with people strolling and sitting in the terraces and restaurants. This is a time when friends meet and enjoy the splendid setting of this beautiful town.

The main place where everyone meets is Riva. From the city of Riva you have a narrow traffic street or the "lower road", towards the place called Dobrota, which is about 7 km long, and is ideal for walkers, bicycle riders as well as for jogging.

During the summer, Prcanj, Stoliv, Perast, and Risan are

especially interesting places. These places are found on both sides of Kotor harbor. It is as if they were made for the lovers of relaxation and quietude. Considering the fact that there are no sandy beaches in Kotor, you can easily get a ride to some of the Tivat beaches by taxi, taxi van, barge or boat. In Tivat the beaches are numerous but we will leave the choice to you. We will only suggest some of them: Plavi horizonti, Kalardovo or Oblatno.

If that is not the destination to which you wish to go, you can go towards Herceg Novi and spend a pleasant summer's day in that town. For swimming and sun bathing outside Kotor, we are of course also suggesting the metropolis of tourism: Budva. From Kotor, the distance to Budva is 25 km and to Herceg Novi 35 km. During the summer season, longer trips are organized by the traveler's ship "Jovan", which during is anchored in Kotor harbor and offers cruising towards Herceg Novi or by road via Tivat and Budva to Bar.

Kotor is also a sports town. It is most famous for water polo, because for a long time they had the water polo school "Primorac". That club owns an indoor Olympic pool and the open pool in the sea which is close to Kotor harbor. In Kotor there is also a football stadium as well as the terrains for other sports.

In recent years, the sailing competition by Kotor has been revived. Regattas are being organized and in the sailing club "Lahor" (Breeze) there are once again many sailors. There is also a diving club "Zubatac" (Dentex) where you can rent all the right gear. Next to the shipping channel of the bay of Boka Kotorska, the water is calm.

Kotor is also an interesting place for the mountain lovers. Towards the peak of Sveti Ivan (St. Ivan), above Kotor, you have a path to enjoy the fun of hiking. The path curves further towards Krstac on the Lovcen mountain (height 965 m), from where you can then go further towards Pestingrad (1098 m) or towards the Jezerski vrh (Lake Peak; 1657 m), the second highest peak on Lovcen, where the magnificent mausoleum of Petra II Petrovic Njegos, a Montenegrin ruler and poet, is situated. Such hikes are organized by the Kotor club "Pestigrad", which is working with great dedication on the development of the free climbing and marking of the paths in Kotor and the surrounding for hiking.

Also, in Kotor itself, there is also a city park beside the sea which has a playground for children and a lot of benches to rest on.

Of all the towns on the Montenegrin coast, when going by the number of cafés, Kotor is number one. Beside the city cafés, Kotor has a great number of terrace cafés, which are mostly situated

along the shore and are especially attractive during the warm summer nights. Although they are most often visited by young people who are craving for entertainment and fast life style, you can also meet plenty of older people who wish to sense the spirit of youth, drink a cappuccino or espresso.

In the vicinity of the Old town, the most famous Kotor discothèque "Secondo porto" is situated, which is visited late at night by young people and those who yearn for contemporary music and dancing. During the summer months, there is also another music venue: discothèque Malibu.

But best night life in Old Town is in huge modern unique discothèque "Maximus" one of the best equipped, and the most attractive discotheques in this part of Europe. Located in the center of the old town of Kotor, is practically built into its walls. 4 stages, until the early morning hours can be enjoyed over 4 000 people. The complex includes lounge bar, piano lounge and pub Mediterraneo..

The traditionally sparkling spirit of the people from Kotor is noticeable in every place in the town and what is most interesting is the loud talk of people from Kotor, when they meet some old and some new friends. That loud talk is known under as CAKULANJE (parley).

The entertainment life in Kotor is made even more special by the great number of music concerts, which are either organized in the museums or old Kotor churches or the halls for concert music playing.

During the summer months, there are a large number of fisherman's fiestas as well as carnivals plus various kinds of entertainment for children, young people and performances for the adults.

Tourism – Top Tours

According to the opinions of the experts, Kotor should develop itself in cultural tourism. During the summer, the Old Town of Kotor is visited by several thousand domestic and foreign tourists. In the last two years, during the tourist season, interesting guest visits came from France. The tourists came aboard the boat "Jason" and via Croatia. They spent their days touring through the Old Town or by buses that are part of the organized excursions, exploring the most interesting parts of Montenegro in that way. Foreign tourists also come to Kotor by the Croatian boat called "Dalmacija".

Similar trips are offered by almost all the domestic tourist agencies in Kotor. The most interesting are the trips to the Montenegrin capital and the historical and cultural nucleus of Montenegro – Cetinje. You also have trips to Ulcinj's Velika plaza (big beach), and Skadar Lake. Numerous agencies or individuals offer visits to

Montenegrin monasteries and churches all over Montenegro. A large number of agencies every day offer the trips to other towns along the Montenegrin coast. We can single out visits to Budva, Bar, Herceg Novi, and Ulcinj. Also, you have interesting tourist arrangements which include a visit to Skadar Lake, famous monasteries and breaks for lunch in interesting restaurants or motels along the way.

Tourist agencies can offer organized travels to Croatia, more specifically to ancient Dubrovnik. The information about these trips can be obtained in the Tourist Organization of Kotor, independent tourist agencies or directly from the owners of the taxi vans and organizers of such travels. You can mostly find them along the city Riva or at the places which are intended for taxi drivers. Also very interesting are cruises with taxi barges or boats to Herceg Novi or Budva, which, if you decide to have such a cruise, is easy to organize from Kotor.

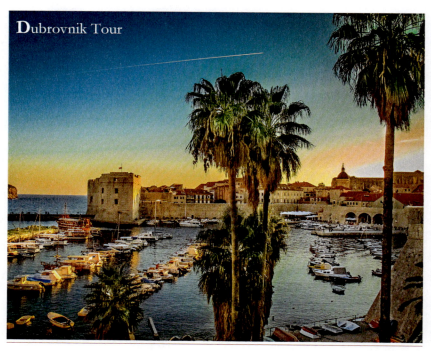

Dubrovnik Tour

Tourism – Churches, Monasteries

What Kotor is most famous for is the Old Town Cathedral of Sveti Tripun (St. Triphon). That temple is mentioned for the first time in the IX century, when the relics of Sveti Tripun, who died in martyrdom in the era of the Roman emperor Decije, in the III century, arrived there. Historians testify that the temple was likely to have disappeared in a fire in the X century but was rebuilt in the XII century. The cathedral of Sveti Tripun was rebuilt in the Romanic style, with the elements of the Byzantium architecture. It survived several earthquakes, so its appearance also changed. Especially visible on the cathedral are the elements of renaissance and Baroque. In 2002, the European Union and the organization Europa Nostra awarded the cathedral a plaque for the great reconstruction and seismic security measures of the oldest Romanic cathedral on the

Adriatic coast. As the most important monument and symbol of the Old Town, the cathedral of Sveti Tripun has a rich treasury of the precious relics among which we have a gilded altar, Baroque frescoes and a large number of ornaments of great value.

The church of Sveti Nikola is the most significant Orthodox Church in Kotor. It is located in the North part of the town and was built at the beginning of the XX century, on the basis of the old edifice which was ruined in a fire in the XIX century. Nearby is the church treasury with a rich collection of icons, artistic crafts, documents and church gowns. The church owns other numerous valuable relics which were mostly given to it by wealthy Kotor families.

The church of Sveti Luka is also situated in the Old Town. It was built during the reign of the Serbian dynasty Nemanjic, at the en of the XII century. Until the middle of the XVII century, the church of Sveti Luka initially was the main Catholic temple. After the war with the Turks, it became an Orthodox Church because the number of the Orthodox people in Kotor suddenly increased. Still, catholic believers had their altar in that temple until the first half of the XIX century.

In the middle part of the Old Town is the church of Sveti Mihailo (St. Michael), which has had its present day appearance since the end of the XIV century. The archeological remains show that on the place of the today's church of Sveti Mihailo, there used to be a significantly larger edifice in the XII century. In the east part of Old Kotor, is the church of Sveta Ana. Considering the fact that it was added onto several times, it can not be determined precisely when was it built. Experts for the reconstruction of the old edifices have still managed to find some of the records showing that the older part of the church of Sveta Ana was built in XIII century and the newer one in the XIV century. The church is characterized by several saints to whom it was dedicated: Sevti Martin, Sveta Venerada and today Sveta Ana.

The interior of the Old Town in Kotor is characterized by the famous church of Sveta Marija Koledjate (The Lady of Health); in Kotor this church is more famous by the name Sveta Ozana. It was built at the beginning of the XIII century. During the centuries, it had several changes. Below the church, researchers have discovered the oldest archeological edifice that was ever found – an early Christian basilica from the VI century. Among the numerous monuments, in the Old Town of Kotor, there are also churches of Sveti Josip (St. Joseph), Gospa od Andjela (Lady of Angels) and Sveti Pavle (St. Pavli).

To all the religious monuments in the Old Town of Kotor, we should also add the city tower which originates from the XVII century, with the pillory in front of it and a clock mechanism which is a part of the edifice. Nearby this tower is also the tower of the city watch, the Prince's Palace and the City Theatre, which was the first theatre that started to work in the XIX century in the Balkans.

Tourism – Palaces

Kotor is also famous for its numerous palaces, which are characterized by the Romanic and Baroque ornaments, wall decorations and a great number of the heraldry of the families from whom the palaces got their names or to whom they belonged.

Among the numerous palaces we have some that stand out. Palace Bizanti, in the Romanic style, is situated next to the Tower of the City watch and it originates from the XIV century. Baroque palace Grgurin is found in the central part of the Old Town. It was built at the beginning of the XVIII century. The famous Kotor family Buca has built a palace Buca in the XIV century, which during the centuries has been added onto several times and later it belonged to the family Pskvali. In the vicinity, we also have one of the most noble city houses, which originate from the XIV century, palace

Vrakjen. That palace has mostly retained its original appearance. In the vicinity of the cathedral Sveti Tripun is palace Drago, which was built in the XV century, in Baroque and Gothic style. Still, according to the opinion of many people, the most beautiful Kotor palace is the palace Pima, which is characteristic by its Gothic style with some Baroque elements. The Pima family, which owned the same named palace, lived in Kotor from XIV to XVIII century. The present day appearance palace dates back to the end of the XVII century.

Porto Montenegro, Tivat Tour

Accommodation in Kotor

Kotor offers a wide range of accommodation. We suggest that you make an ONLINE BOOKING because this is best way to get a great price as well as good accommodation. The Online Booking service does not only offer expensive hotels. You can find many small private apartments with great service and affordable prices.

We present you here with a short list of some hotels in Kotor (188 accommodation units, from May 2014):

Vu De' Hostel

Accommodation Marija 2

Apartman More

Apartman na Pjaci od muzeja

Apartmani Cetkovic

Apartmani Kovacevic

Apartmani Novakovic

Apartmani Saxo

Apartmant Beachfront

Apartment Anja

Apartment Athos

Apartment Barba

Apartment D&D

Apartment Dejo

Apartment Exclusive

Apartment Filip

Apartment Gigi

Apartment Gogo

Apartment Ivaniševic 2

Apartment Jankovic

Apartment Jankovic

Apartment Jovicevic

Apartment Kaludjerovic 2

Apartment Kristina

Apartment Marko

Apartment Palata Bizanti

Apartment Pavle

Apartment Sara

Apartment Sunny View

Apartment Vanja

Apartment Vjera

Apartment Vukasovic

Apartment Vukotic 2

Apartments Anapaola

Apartments Babilon

Apartments Bella di Mare

Apartments Bella Vista

Apartments Bogdanovic

Apartments Brajic-Radanovici

Apartments Brguljan

Apartments Coral

Apartments Corovic

Apartments Coso

Apartments Cosovic

Apartments Dakovic

Apartments Dakovic M

Apartments Dani

Apartments Djordje Dobrota

Apartments Djuranovic

Apartments Djurovic

Apartments Dobriša

Apartments Doncic

Apartments Feniks

Apartments Iva

Apartments Ivaniševic

Apartments Ivanovic

Apartments Ivardic

Apartments Ivetic

Apartments Jokovic

Apartments Jovanovic

Apartments Kaludjerovic

Apartments Kavac

Apartments Kordic

Apartments Kotor Sunrise

Apartments Kriva Ulica

Apartments Lara

Apartments Lea

Apartments Luka

Apartments Marilu

Apartments Markovic

Apartments Matkovic

Apartments Meša

Apartments Meštrovic

Apartments Mihovic

Apartments Milunovic

Apartments Miramar

Apartments Moskov

Apartments Nancy

Apartments Nikcevic

Apartments Nima

Apartments Paradiso

Apartments Parteli

Apartments Pejanovic

Apartments Penovic Stoliv Bay Kotor

Apartments Popovic

Apartments Prcanj

Apartments Radimir

Apartments Radojkovic

Apartments Radonicic

Apartments Radonjic

Apartments Radulovic

Apartments Roganovic

Apartments Rozer

Apartments S&P -

Apartments Saint Stasije

Apartments Samardzic

Apartments Sandra

Apartments Sara & Barbara

Apartments Simun

Apartments Sole Luna

Apartments Sonja

Apartments Soso

Apartments Vasilije

Apartments Villa Dobrota

Apartments Villa Ferri

Apartments Villa Marta

Apartments Vojvoda

Apartments Vukasovic

Apartments Vukotic I

Apartments Vukovic

Apartments Vuksanovic

Apartments Wine House Old Town

Apartments Zeljko

Apartments Zenit

Apartments Zvijezda Mora

Apartments Djukic

Apartments Djurovic

Art Hotel Galathea

B & M Apartments

Bastion Apartment

Bjelica Apartments Kotor

Boutique Hotel Astoria

Cattaro Lux Apartment

Citrus Studios

Cottage House With Sea View

D & Sons Apartments

Dekaderon Lux Apartments

Donkovic Accommodation

Gardenia Studios

Guest House Forza Lux

Guest House Jelena

Guest House Šljuka

Guest House Tomcuk

Guesthouse Anita

Guesthouse Tianis

Hajdana Apartments

Holiday Home Villa Andrea

Hostel Old Town Kotor

Hotel Bokeljski Dvori

Hotel Casa del Mare - Amfora

Hotel Cattaro

Hotel Forza Mare

Hotel Galia

Hotel Hippocampus

Hotel Marija

Hotel Monte Cristo

Hotel Pana

Hotel Rendez Vous

Hotel Splendido

Hotel Vardar

Hotel Villa Duomo

J & P Apartments

Kamena Palata Apartments

Kotor Bay Apartments & Houses Evkowski

Kotor Tianis Apartments

La Grande Apartments

Lanterna Apartments

Ljuta Studios

Montenegro Hostel Kotor

Muo Apartments

Nikolic Guesthouse

Old Mariner Guest House

Old Town Boskovic Apartment

Palazzo Drusko Deluxe Rooms

Palazzo Radomiri

Palma Apartments

Panorama Rooms

Rooms Dobrotski Dvori

Savic Apartments

Studio Aki

Studio Dragan

Studios Kono

Studios Radanovic

Studios Vuckovic

Sunset Apartments

V&T Apartments

VG Three Bedroom Castle

Vicky Apartments

Vila "PM"

Vila Panonija

Vila Prcanj

Villa Duja

Villa Feja

Villa Iva

Villa Ivana

Villa Zvicer

Vjera Apartments

Waterfront Apartments

ONLINE BOOKING ON: www.visit-montenegro.com

---

* * * * * * * *

We also recommend you to check this best on-line booking service on for updated information about all available hotels in Kotor and other destination: **ONLINE BOOKING on Visit-Montenegro.com**

Also, if you want to use rental car service, we recommend : **ONLINE RENTAL CAR SERVICE on Visit-Montenegro. com**

If you have some specific demands, we recommend to contact: **VISIT MONTENEGRO (www.visit-montenegro.com)**

Kotor Map

In this edition, we provide couple of very nice, useful maps of Kotor Old Town. Map with marked churches and palaces, Map with quick walk tour and Map with long walk tour. With this maps, you will be able to find and visit all main points in Kotor Old Town.

For more information and more maps:

Google Kotor Map

City map provided by Google Map Service is best for make complete impression of Kotor city.

Accommodation Kotor Map

This is great interactive map with all available accommodation in Kotor. With one click you can get all information about every hotel, motel, apartment, see prices and make online booking. This map can be found on Visit-Montenegro.com

Paper Maps in Visit Montenegro Shop

In this online shop, you can find and order many paper materials from Montenegro, like maps, guides, books, postcards, souvenirs, etc. Official Visit Montenegro Shop is on url: shop.visit-montenegro.com

Finally, when you visit Kotor, you will be able to buy many maps or brochures of Old Town and whole Kotor city in many small Tourist Shops in Old Town Kotor.

KOTOR OLD TOWN MAP

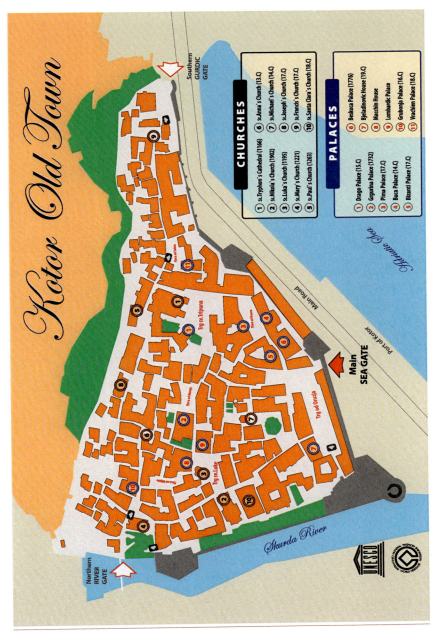

KOTOR OLD TOWN - QUICK WALK TOUR

Kotor Old Town

TOUR - 1

QUICK WALK TOUR

△ GATES   ▬▬ TOUR PATH   RAMPARTS

1. Weapon MAIN Square, Bizanti Palace
2. Flour Square, Pima Palace
3. St.Tryphon`s Cathedral, Drago Palace
4. Musemus Square
5. St.Luka, St.Nikola, Macchin, Lombardic Palace
6. St Michael Church
7. Bjeladinovic House (Main Sqaure)

Southern GURDIC GATE

Main SEA GATE

Northern RIVER GATE

Adriatic Sea

Port of Kotor

Main Road

Skurda River

UNESCO

KOTOR OLD TOWN - LONG WALK TOUR

Kotor Old Town

TOUR - 2

LONG WALK TOUR

◀ GATES ◀ TOUR PATH ◀ RAMPARTS

1 Weapon (main) Square
2 Bjeladinovic House,
3 St.Clara, St.Nikola,
4 St.Luka Church,
5 Macchin House,
6 St.Marry Church,
7 Grubonja Palace,
8 St. Anna Church,
9 Grgurina Palace,
10 St.Joseph Church,
11 St. Paul Church,
12 St. Fransis Church,
13 Vrachien Palace,
14 St. Tryphon, Drago Plc.
15 Pima & Buca Palaces,
16 Bizanti & Beskura Plcs.
17 St.Michael Church,
18 Weapon (main) Square

Southern GURDIC GATE

Main SEA GATE

Main Road

Port of Kotor

Trg sv. Tripuna

Skurda River

Northern RIVER GATE

UNESCO

Visit Montenegro Digital Edition

Visit-Montenegro.com, the leading web portal for Montenegro, is the first site that is publishing useful digital books and digital tourist guides.

You can find all the information you need about Montenegro and all main tourist destinations in Montenegro are listed. There is also a wide range of articles and information as well as many splendid and unique photos, maps and links. Each digital edition is a great companion for every tourist who wants to visit and have great holiday in Montenegro.

We wish that you to enjoy our digital edition and to have given you the best impression about all aspects of Montenegro. All your comments and suggestions are welcome

Montenegro - Breathtaking Beauty

My Notes About Kotor

51328791R00037

Made in the USA
San Bernardino, CA
19 July 2017